Who Is
Harry Styles?

Who Is Harry Styles?

by Kirsten Anderson

illustrated by Andrew Thomson

Penguin Workshop

To Rhia, Cerys, and soon-to-be
New Baby Thomson—AT

PENGUIN WORKSHOP
An imprint of Penguin Random House LLC, New York

First published in the United States of America by Penguin Workshop,
an imprint of Penguin Random House LLC, New York, 2023

Visit us online at penguinrandomhouse.com.

Library of Congress Cataloging-in-Publication Data is available.

Printed in the United States of America

ISBN 9780593662656 (paperback)   10 9 8 7 6 5 4 3 2 1 WOR
ISBN 9780593750117 (library binding)   10 9 8 7 6 5 4 3 2 1 WOR

Contents

Who Is Harry Styles?

"What's your name?"

Simon Cowell, a judge on the TV talent show *The X Factor UK*, stared sternly at the young man standing onstage.

"I'm Harry Styles."

"How old are you?"

"I'm sixteen."

Harry was one of the youngest contestants to audition for the British show that year. He loved to sing but had no idea if he was any good. He was in a small band with friends, and his mom, Anne, always encouraged him. But auditioning for *The X Factor UK* would give him a chance to get a professional opinion. If the show's judges liked him, maybe he could make music his career.

So, in March of 2010, Harry's family made the three-hour journey to London, where they waited with Harry alongside thousands of other hopeful performers. Harry sang for several assistants and producers, and they kept passing him through to the next level. Only the best singers would get a chance to audition in front of the judges and a live audience. Harry was one of the ones who made it that far.

Harry answered Simon's questions about the bakery where he worked on Saturdays. There was a reason behind the somewhat random questions. They were meant to show whether a performer could speak confidently under pressure, without showing any nerves. *The X Factor UK* was based on the idea that true stars weren't just talented. They had a special "something" that grabbed people's attention. Some people call this "the X factor." Based on Harry's comfort onstage, and the way the audience cheered for him, it sure seemed like he might have that "something."

But he also had to show them that he could sing.

Harry started to sing a song by the band Train, along with recorded music. But Simon stopped him quickly and said he thought that the recorded music was throwing Harry off.

He asked if Harry could sing something else. Harry began to sing "Isn't She Lovely" by Stevie Wonder, but without any recorded music playing. This time he seemed more confident. Now the judges had to decide whether he should move on to the next phase of the show or not.

Louis Walsh, another judge, said he liked Harry but thought he was too young. The audience booed Louis loudly. Judge Nicole Scherzinger voted for Harry to move on. Now it was up to Simon Cowell. He was known as the tough judge, but he knew how to find talent and turn people into stars. He voted yes. The audience cheered and screamed. Harry was going on to the next part of the competition.

The audience was right to cheer. This performance was the start of something huge! Soon Harry Styles would be one of the biggest stars in the world thanks to his choice to audition for the competition that day. It all started when five teenagers from *The X Factor UK* were brought together to create one of the biggest boy bands in history.

CHAPTER 1
Finding the X Factor

Harry Edward Styles was born on February 1, 1994, in Redditch, Worcestershire, England, to his parents, Anne Twist and Desmond Styles. He has an older sister, Gemma. The family later moved to Holmes Chapel in the northwestern part of England, near Manchester. When Harry was seven years old, his parents decided to divorce. While he spent most of his time with his mother, his father was still involved in his life.

Harry grew up listening to the music that his parents played during car rides. Their favorites, like Fleetwood Mac, the Rolling Stones, and Shania Twain, became his favorites, too. Harry soon discovered that he loved to sing.

Family 1997

He often clowned around while performing in front of people, imitating singers like Elvis Presley. But he was too shy to really sing in his own voice in public. He saved those private performances for home, where only Gemma could hear Harry singing to himself.

As a teen, Harry got bolder about singing. He formed a band with friends from school, and they entered a local Battle of the Bands— and won! Harry loved the experience and began to wonder if he could become a professional singer.

In 2010, Anne heard that there were going to be auditions in London for *The X Factor UK*, a singing competition. She filled out the application for Harry and he agreed to go. But as it got closer to the date, Harry became so nervous that he got sick. He still decided to go to the audition.

After Harry made it through the first audition,

he and the other singers were sent to "boot camp" where they learned new songs and dances, then performed for the judges again. Only the top singers from the group would move on to the next part of the competition. On July 23, 2010, Harry stood onstage with all the other boys, hoping to hear his name called. When it wasn't, he was crushed. He didn't want to just go back home and go back to school. It felt like his dream had come to an end.

Then, just as Harry was getting ready to leave, a producer asked several boys to come back onstage. Harry was one of them. He wasn't excited about it. Harry thought the producers probably just wanted to interview them and film them crying to add some drama to the show. But he was very, very wrong.

Behind the scenes, the judges had struggled deciding which boys should move on. Judge Nicole Scherzinger began to put some of them together to compete as a group instead of as solo singers. One of the group members was Harry.

The five boys waited onstage and listened as Scherzinger explained the group idea to them.

Harry and the other boys jumped around, celebrating. He hardly knew them, but Niall Horan, Liam Payne, Louis Tomlinson, and Zayn Malik were about to become some of the most important people in Harry's life.

CHAPTER 2
Third-Place Winners

The boys had a few weeks off before they began the next phase of the competition. They realized that they needed to spend time with each other and learn how to sing as a group. Harry's mother's boyfriend owned a small cottage, and he invited the boys to stay there.

During those weeks, the new band members got to know each other. They talked, joked, and listened to music. They came up with band names, and Harry suggested One Direction. That sounded good to everyone.

By the time One Direction got to the next part of the competition, they looked more like a group of friends than five strangers who had been thrown together. And they sang well, too.

The new band was sent to the biggest part of the competition. Each week, they would have to learn a new song and perform live in front of an audience. Then, voters would call in from all over the United Kingdom to decide who should move on to the next round—and who should be sent home.

They moved into a house in London with all the other *X Factor UK* contestants and started working on new songs to perform. Harry got very nervous before the first show but made it through the band's performance of "Viva La Vida" by Coldplay. One Direction received enough votes to keep going.

Each week, the band got better and better. But something else was happening, too.

At first there were a few fans waiting for them outside the *X Factor UK* studio. People who saw One Direction on the show began to post photos and news about them on social

media, and uploaded clips from *The X Factor
UK* on YouTube. Soon there were hundreds of
fans waiting to see the boys. When the show

One Direction performs "Viva La Vida"

sent them out for promotional appearances, even more fans showed up.

It wasn't just their singing or good looks that attracted fans. *X Factor UK* contestants had to record video diaries for the show, where the boys talked about their week and answered fan questions. These videos gave them a chance to be silly and have fun. Audiences loved how relatable and funny the young men in One Direction were. People could imagine being friends with them.

Finally, on December 10, 2010, One Direction was eliminated from *The X Factor UK*. Overall, they finished third in the competition. The band members were devastated. But One Direction wasn't finished. In early 2011, One Direction signed a contract with Simon's music label, SYCO Music. By April, the band was in a professional recording studio, singing original songs written just for them.

In August, their first song, "What Makes You Beautiful," was released, followed by a music video filmed on a beach in California. It showed how different One Direction was from other boy bands at the time. Most other boy bands dressed alike and performed tightly choreographed dances. But in One Direction's first video, they mostly just played around on the beach, like a group of friends hanging out together. Fans everywhere wanted to join them.

Boy Bands!

Every few years, a new boy band captures the hearts of a new group of fans. Here are a few of the most famous boy bands.

NAME	FROM	MOST POPULAR YEARS
Menudo	Puerto Rico	1977–2009
New Edition	Boston, MA	1984–1997
New Kids on the Block	Boston, MA	1988–1994
Backstreet Boys	Orlando, FL	1996–2009
*NSYNC	Orlando, FL	1995–2002
BTS	Seoul, South Korea	2013–

BTS performing live

FAMOUS MEMBERS	HITS
Miguel Cancel, René Farrait, Johnny Lozada, Ricky Martin, Charlie Masso, Ricky Meléndez, Ray Reyes, Xavier Serbiá	"Quiero Ser" ("I Want to Be") "Súbete A Mi Moto" ("Get on My Motorcycle")
Ricky Bell, Michael Bivins, Bobby Brown, Ronnie DeVoe, Johnny Gill, Ralph Tresvant	"Cool It Now" "Mr. Telephone Man" "If It Isn't Love"
Jonathan Knight, Jordan Knight, Joey McIntyre, Donnie Wahlberg, Danny Wood	"You Got It (The Right Stuff)" "Step By Step"
Nick Carter, Howie Dorough, Brian Littrell, AJ McLean, Kevin Richardson	"Quit Playing Games (With My Heart)" "Larger Than Life" "I Want It That Way"
Lance Bass, JC Chasez, Joey Fatone, Chris Kirkpatrick, Justin Timberlake	"Bye Bye Bye" "This I Promise You" "It's Gonna Be Me"
J-Hope, Jimin, Jin, Jungkook, RM, Suga, V	"Dynamite" "Butter" "Permission to Dance"

CHAPTER 3
One Direction

The band traveled all over England and Europe, performing "What Makes You Beautiful" to fast-growing audiences. Soon, the song topped the music charts in a number of countries. When One Direction's first album, *Up All Night*, was released in the United Kingdom in November 2011, it entered the charts at number two and became the country's fastest-selling debut album of the year.

Soon, it was time for their first live performances in the United States. On March 12, 2012, One Direction was scheduled to perform on *Today*, the popular US morning show. Over fifteen thousand fans swarmed around the outdoor stage in Rockefeller Center in New

York City. *Today* had never drawn a crowd this big for a new band . . . and *Up All Night* hadn't even come out in the United States yet!

When the album was released in the United States on March 13, it went straight to number one on the *Billboard* music charts. One Direction was the first British band to have their debut album land in the number one spot in the US charts.

One Direction toured the United States. In August 2012, they performed at the Summer Olympics closing ceremony in London. In between all the touring, they recorded a whole new album. *Take Me Home* was released in November 2012.

Before setting off on their next tour, One Direction was asked to record a song for Comic Relief, a charity event that raises money for children living in poverty. One Direction traveled to Ghana to film a video to go with the song. They had the opportunity to visit children in schools and hospitals. Harry described the experience as "the most amazing day" in his life ever.

Harry had fun traveling the world with the band. But he also worried a lot. He was scared that he might sing a wrong note or make a mistake during a show. And One Direction's record contract stated that the contract could end immediately if he did or said anything the record company didn't like. He feared doing anything that might ruin his career or hurt the band. He expected a lot from himself.

Fans, who called themselves Directioners, expected a lot from the band, too. They formed a strong community that supported everything One Direction did. They live streamed One Direction's concerts and created social media accounts devoted to the band. Groups of fans

organized to buy multiple copies of albums and watched music videos over and over to help them break records for their number of views.

Critics often dismissed One Direction. They thought that One Direction just made simple music for teen girls who liked cute boys. But Harry thought that was wrong. He later told an interviewer that those girls' opinions were important, because they were the future leaders, doctors, and lawyers of the world.

Charming and funny, Harry became a fan favorite. He appreciated the fans and knew they were the ones who had made One Direction a success. But now, everyone was watching him. When he went on a date, it became international news. And when certain fans didn't like a woman he dated, some would make vicious comments about her online.

Fans always wanted more, so One Direction kept going. They recorded albums and then toured to support the album. There were TV appearances and interviews. The band made commercials for brands, including Pepsi, Colgate, and Honda. They even released a collection of perfumes.

In between everything, Harry worked on becoming a more well-rounded musician. He started taking piano lessons, and his bandmate Niall taught him how to play the guitar. The third One Direction album, *Midnight Memories*

(2013), featured more songs written by the band members, including Harry. But he felt he wasn't getting the full songwriting experience. He would write parts of songs, but then he would have to go on tour again and other songwriters would finish them. He wanted to do more, but there was never enough time.

In 2014, *Four* became One Direction's fourth album in a row to debut at number one on the charts, something no other group had done. One Direction seemed to be on top of the world.

Then, on March 25, 2015, just as the band was beginning a new tour, Zayn Malik quit. At first, the other members of One Direction were shocked and a little bit angry. They still had a whole tour ahead of them, and they were already planning another album.

The tour continued with just Niall, Liam, Louis, and Harry. Still, something had changed.

Harry had loved being in One Direction, but he wanted to try out new things. So did the others. On August 23, 2015, One Direction announced that it was going on hiatus, or taking a break. The last live show of their tour took place in Sheffield, England, on October 31, 2015. One Direction's last album, *Made in the A.M.*, which was recorded without Zayn, was released in November.

And then, for the first time since 2010, Harry was on his own.

CHAPTER 4
Solo Act

Harry hadn't known exactly what he wanted to do after One Direction went on break. But he had enjoyed acting in school, and thought he'd like to try it again.

It was perfect timing. Director Christopher Nolan was making a movie about the Battle of Dunkirk. He wanted actors who were young and inexperienced, just like the soldiers who fought in the real World War II battle in 1940. Nolan didn't know much about Harry, but he liked his audition and thought he had an "old-fashioned face," as if he could have lived in the 1940s. Nolan cast Harry as one of the British soldiers stranded on the coast of France.

Dunkirk, which was filmed on the French beach where the actual battle took place, was a massive production. One day Harry would be sitting on a beach with vintage fighter planes buzzing overhead, the next he was swimming in the cold water of the English Channel while boats blew up nearby. It was unlike anything Harry had ever done.

After filming finished, Harry was ready to get back to music. His first solo record contract was very different from the one he had signed with One Direction. It didn't say Harry had to be careful about what he did or said. When he noticed that, he was so relieved that he cried. Harry hadn't realized how much the other contract had controlled him until that moment. Now he felt he could really be free.

For his first solo album, Harry wanted to really dive fully into the songwriting process and be part of everything from beginning to end.

He wasn't sure what kind of music he wanted to make as a solo artist, and he didn't want people telling him what he should sound like. So, he put together a new band and gathered producers he knew. He brought them to a house in Jamaica. They spent two months there, just playing music and testing out different types of songs. Harry discovered that he really loved spending time in a studio and being creative.

Harry's first solo album, *Harry Styles*, was released in May 2017. It debuted at number one on the charts in the United Kingdom, the United States, and Australia. Critics were impressed by the album, and when Harry announced the dates for his first solo tour, the shows sold out almost immediately. Touring as a solo singer for the first time changed Harry. He hadn't been sure whether fans just liked One Direction, or if they would like his new music, too. But when he heard audiences singing his new songs back at him, he felt accepted. He realized his fans wanted him to truly be himself. He would remember that as he started to think about writing his next album.

Dunkirk premiered in theaters in July 2017.

It was a success at the box office and got excellent reviews. Many critics were surprised by Harry's performance. They felt he was believable as the young soldier and thought he showed skill as an actor.

After the tour ended, Harry spent some time in early 2019 living in Tokyo, one of his favorite cities. He passed his days reading in cafés and listening to music at record shops. Most people didn't even notice him, and he appreciated the quiet time. When Harry went to work on his next album, he was feeling more secure and ready to experiment. This time, he tried out a new sound and wrote lyrics that felt more personal and honest.

When *Fine Line* was released in December 2019, it debuted at number three on the UK charts and number one in the United States. Harry planned a tour that was set to begin in April 2020.

Then, in March 2020, the COVID-19 pandemic shut down much of the world. Harry had been in a cycle of recording and touring almost nonstop since 2011. But now, there was nothing he could do but stop and wait.

CHAPTER 5
Harry's World

Harry was in Los Angeles, California, when pandemic lockdowns began. He moved in with friends, and they spent the next few months just hanging out, talking, and watching movies together. It was the first time in years that Harry had a chance to spend long periods of time with friends. Harry had wondered if he could be happy when he wasn't performing. He wasn't sure who he would be without music. But now he realized that he could be creative because he wanted to, not because music was all he had.

Soon Harry started to write again. When he heard that a nearby studio was available, he got together with his producers and band and recorded a new album. He called it *Harry's*

Harry in the studio working on *Harry's House*

House and described the songs on the album as his thoughts during a day in his life. He hoped to capture the feeling of being at home.

After watching a lot of movies during the lockdown, Harry thought he might like to act again. He auditioned for a movie called *Don't Worry Darling* but didn't get the part. But when the actor who was originally cast left the film, they offered the part to Harry. He spent several months filming in California.

In March 2021, the Grammy Awards, one of the music industry's biggest awards, were given out. Harry won Best Pop Solo performance for the song "Watermelon Sugar" from the album *Fine Line*. It was his first Grammy Award.

Harry got into more acting roles. He was cast in the starring role of a new dramatic movie called *My Policeman*. Marvel fans were surprised when Harry was cast as Eros, the brother of supervillain Thanos.

Harry loved acting, but he really missed recording music and performing in front of audiences. The tour that had been postponed due to the pandemic was set to begin in September 2021, and Harry was ready to get back in front of a crowd.

In December 2020, Harry had appeared on the cover of *Vogue* magazine wearing a dress. He had been including clothes usually associated with women in his outfits for several years, and some people began to ask questions about his fashion choices. Harry explained that he thought fashion should be fun. He felt that people should wear what they wanted and that labeling clothes as male or female was an outdated idea. In November 2021, he introduced Pleasing, his own line of personal care products like nail polish and makeup that were meant for anyone, regardless of gender.

As Harry resumed touring and performing concerts, his fans began to copy his unique style. When he wore a feather boa, his fans began to wear them, too. Like Harry, they wore glitter and sequins. "Harryween," Harry's shows scheduled around Halloween, suddenly became big events. At one performance, he and his band dressed like clowns. At another, they dressed like characters from *The Wizard of Oz*, with Harry as Dorothy.

Harry tries to make everyone feel included at his concerts, and he interacts with his fans as much as he can. He has joined fans in supporting racial justice movements such as Black Lives Matter and has helped LGBTQ+ fans come out (share their sexual orientation and gender identity openly) to their families during his shows. He talks about the importance of mental health with fans and has explained how therapy has helped him.

When "As It Was," the first single from *Harry's House*, was released in April 2022, it became a number one hit. *Harry's House* was released on May 20, 2022. That night, Harry performed a special "One Night Only" concert in New York, where he played the new album from beginning to end. At the end of the show, he told the audience how grateful he was to them and thanked them for changing his life.

Harry's House became one of the best-selling albums of 2022. It went on to win three Grammy Awards, including Best Pop Vocal Album and Album of the Year.

Harry has called himself a "perfectionist" but tries to make sure that doesn't keep him from trying new things. He's learned that if he thinks something sounds scary, he should probably do it. When he writes songs, he has found that when he is truly honest, that makes

Harry at the 2023 Grammy Awards

his songs better. Even if that can scare him a little bit.

Harry Styles has been famous for most of his life, which isn't easy. He's learned that it's okay to find a balance between the work he loves and being a good friend, son, and brother. Being nice also helps. During his first solo tour, Harry put a pin on his guitar strap that said "Treat People with Kindness," and that became a slogan for the tour. On *Fine Line*, he included a song also titled "Treat People with Kindness." Harry explained that it's about how "small changes end up making a big difference. It's about being a lot nicer to each other."

Harry's life has changed so much since he was a nervous sixteen-year-old auditioning for a television show. But his dedication to small acts of kindness is something he won't soon outgrow. And his fans love him for it.

Timeline of Harry Styles's Life

1994 — Harry Styles is born on February 1 in Redditch, Worcestershire, England

2010 — Auditions for *The X Factor UK* and becomes part of boy band One Direction

2011 — First One Direction album, *Up All Night*, is released, followed by tour

2012 — One Direction album *Take Me Home* is released, followed by tour

2013 — One Direction album *Midnight Memories* is released, followed by tour

2014 — One Direction album *Four* is released, followed by tour the next year

2015 — One Direction announces hiatus and releases the *Made in the A.M.* album

2017 — First solo album, *Harry Styles*, is released

— First movie, *Dunkirk*, is released

— Begins first solo tour

2019 — Releases second solo album, *Fine Line*

2021 — Wins first Grammy Award

— Begins tour for *Fine Line*

2022 — Releases third solo album, *Harry's House*

— Appears in movies *Don't Worry Darling* and *My Policeman*

Timeline of the World

1994	The Channel Tunnel, an underwater railway beneath the English Channel, connecting England and France, opens
2001	British singing talent show *Pop Idol* premieres
2006	Social media site Twitter is launched
2010	Burj Khalifa, the world's tallest building, opens in Dubai
2012	Hurricane Sandy strikes the East Coast of the United States, causing $70.2 billion in damage.
2013	Bombs kill 3 people and injure at least 264 during the Boston Marathon
2014	Germany wins the World Cup
2016	English musician David Bowie dies on January 10
	American musician Prince dies on April 21
2018	Scientists invent a treatment that helps burn victims regrow skin
2019	Fire seriously damages the Notre-Dame Cathedral in Paris
2020	The COVID-19 pandemic strikes
2021	NASA rover *Perseverance* lands on Mars
2022	Elizabeth II, Queen of England, dies on September 8

Bibliography

Aurand, Calvin, and Paul Dugdale, dir. *Harry Styles: Behind the Album*. Columbia Records, 2017.

Bowles, Hamish. "Playtime with Harry Styles." *Vogue*. November 13, 2020. https://www.vogue.com/article/harry-styles-cover-december-2020.

Crowe, Cameron. "Harry Styles' New Direction." *Rolling Stone*. April 18, 2017. https://www.rollingstone.com/music/music-features/harry-styles-new-direction-119432/.

Paul, Larisha. "10 Years of One Direction: The Story of the World's Biggest Boy Band, Told With the Fans Who Made It Happen." *Billboard*. July 16, 2020. https://www.billboard.com/music/pop/one-direction-ten-year-anniversary-fan-interviews-9419436/.

Sheffield, Rob. "The Eternal Sunshine of Harry Styles." *Rolling Stone*. August 26, 2019. https://www.rollingstone.com/music/music-features/harry-styles-cover-interview-album-871568/.

Sherman, Maria. *Larger Than Life: A History of Boy Bands from NKOTB to BTS*. New York: Black Dog & Leventhal Publishers, 2020.

Spanos, Brittany. "Harry's House: How Harry Styles Became the World's Most Wanted Man." *Rolling Stone*. August 22, 2022. https://www.rollingstone.com/music/music-features/harry-styles-harrys-house-dont-worry-darling-my-policeman-cover-1397290/.

Spurlock, Morgan, dir. *One Direction: This Is Us*. Sony Pictures Entertainment, 2013.

Stoppard, Lou. "Finding Home: Harry Styles Reveals the Meaning Behind His New Album, *Harry's House*." *Better Homes & Gardens*. April 26, 2022.

Tiffany, Kaitlin. *Everything I Need I Get From You: How Fangirls Created the Internet as We Know It*. New York: Farrar, Straus and Giroux, 2022.

Winston, Ben, and Dee Koppang O'Leary, dir. *One Direction: A Year in the Making*. ITV2, 2011.

YOUR HEADQUARTERS FOR HISTORY

Activities, Mad Libs, and sidesplitting jokes!
Discover the Who HQ books beyond the biographies